SUPERNATURAL BUSINESS

INVITING THE
POWER OF GOD
INTO THE MARKETPLACE

ALICE BRIGGS
SENECA SCHURBON

ISBN-13: 978-1-7333795-4-0

Contents

Introduction

WELCOME! WE'RE SO glad you're here. And because you are, I'm going to make a couple of assumptions about you. You probably either want to start a business and want to partner with God while you do so, or you already have a business and want to increase divine activity in and around it. Or maybe you have a ministry but want to make sure the fundamentals are in place to manage that ministry well.

You've come to the right place.

And maybe with all the crazy in the world, you want more control and autonomy over yourself and your life than is possible in a traditional career path. We've all experienced a lot of change in 2020 and 2021, and more may be coming. This can be a great opportunity for advancement and success for those able to follow God's lead and tap into his supernatural wisdom and revelation.

Seneca and I have more than eighty years of experience between us in sales, side hustles, and businesses, starting from when we were kids. It took me longer than Seneca to recognize that was God's design for my life. I always hated selling other people's stuff for band and clubs and all the things, which held me back from going into business as an adult. Recognizing the enemy's lies has been critical in making progress in the areas where God's gifted and called me.

I wasn't created to run a business the regular way, but could I connect my abilities with God's wisdom and guidance for a supernatural business? Yes, please!

Throughout this book, Seneca and I pool our expertise and help you partner your business with God so you can have a supernatural business. And if you have a ministry, the bones and guts of a ministry are very similar to those of a business. You'll still want a website, want to share what you have to offer with your target audience, etc. Your tax status may differ, but you still want to manage your resources well.

Both Seneca and I provide services as well as products. We both work with Christians as well as those who don't believe as we do. We both have online businesses although I also regularly work with people in person as well. We both seek to better the lives of our customers and clients through what we offer.

If you've been through other business and marketing books and courses, most of that training has probably been from the "how to get people to buy my stuff" school of thought. We want to create services and products that solve problems from a kingdom perspective and that provide a great life for us as well. Our desire through all that we do and offer is to help people achieve what God gifted and called them to do.

As we did this, we've had to confront a lot of false beliefs in ourselves as well as in the culture at large, and we've blazed a trail for you to follow that will be easier for you than it was for us. We love that, and we hope you rise to the highest heights of your gifting and calling.

Will we cover some of the general basics? Yes, of course. But we're going to tune in with God for his desire for our websites, marketing, goal setting, and more. It's a wild adventure, and we're so glad you've decided to come along with us!

This book was birthed out of a five day challenge that we do, available on our website: www.SupernaturalBiz.com. This book stands on its own, but only video can communicate some aspects clearly. For those, we may refer you to the videos and the online class. That's optional, but we'd love to see you there. Here's a coupon code to get you free access: Iboughtthebook.

Are you ready to get started? Let's go!

SUPERNATURAL
BUSINESS

CHAPTER 1

Supercharging Your
Products and Services

WE'RE GOING TO start out with some of what we've done in our own businesses in order to bring God into our process in a greater way so that we can get bigger results for our clients and customers. This section is an abbreviated version of our in-class video, so if you'd rather listen than read, see what we're talking about, and have this information in a more conversational format, it's available for free at SupernaturalBiz.com. Again, that coupon code to get in free is: Iboughtthebook.

Seneca found her supernatural business when she was about five years old, then dismissed it as "stupid kid stuff" only to pick it back up later in her mid-twenties. She then realized that she could apply some keys from the creation process in Genesis in her own creation process that made all the difference in the world as far as product quality, her belief in the product, and God's ability to work through a physical product.

Alice is an artist, graphic designer, inner healer, and author. God is definitely a part of the inner healing practice, but she found he also works through art.

Alice:

I paint live sometimes at different events, and I once heard that the meaning of a specific painting was that you need to ask God for what you want. I've had some health struggles over the last five or six years. So I thought, *Okay. Well, I'm asking for healing.*

I got home late from the event. I've struggled majorly with fatigue, so it took me a couple of days to bring the painting in the house. But as soon as I brought it in, I noticed a shift in my energy level and my health. So I was giving the painting the side-eye, wondering, *What just happened here?*

Then I wondered, *Is this healing transferable?* For it to work, I would need to send out prints. So I did a simple experiment. I had people buy prints, then write down what they were asking God for. I didn't ask for specifics because I didn't need details. But if they asked for something, did they notice a shift? And nearly everybody reported back, which is highly unusual for surveys. Nearly everybody had a shift toward a breakthrough in their life from the time they received the painting and put it up somewhere they could see it. Some people had breakthroughs in more than one area. I asked them about different categories—finances, health, and relationships. A lot of people were contending for more than one area and noticed specific progress.

Seneca:

I create these custom combo consultations for people through phone calls or email. I'll help them with what they need and make them a special combination. (You can see them here: https://www.freedom-flowers.com/custom-flower-essence-blends/)

This lady wanted a combo to help her lose some weight. So we talked on the phone and discussed what she thought the root problem was. She was dealing with some emotional issues. So I made this combo for her and sent it off. Three months later, she made another appointment because she thought the formula needed to be tweaked. When I called here, the first thing she said was, "Hello, Seneca, I've lost one hundred pounds since we last talked."

I responded, "Wow. That's a whole person!"

Don't come to me if you want to lose one hundred pounds in three months. That's not the point. That was just God overriding the limits of my product and my service. I didn't pray and hear the exact right way to formulate this product for her although I do my best. That was God doing God's thing because both of us invited him into the process. He added his "super" onto my "natural" and onto her natural as well.

Alice:
And I think that's the key. That's just like with my "Ask" painting (You can see it here: https://alicearlene.com/shop/angel/ask/) and other projects. Changes happened when I intentionally asked God into that process. He's almost more gentlemanly than I would like. He wants to be invited into that process, and part of the learning curve is that he wants to work with you; he doesn't just want to do everything for you because he enjoys working with you and using your skills and gifts.

Seneca:
I have a binder with my different products in it, and each has a page with a prayer template. These aren't fully scripted prayers but just bullet points that I make sure to include. I intended these to be for employees and the boots-on-the-ground people in other countries associated with my company

so that we would have some consistency, continuity, and agreement. So we're doing a combination of bullet points and winging it. And we're praying in tongues when the English runs out or when that product doesn't have a page. But in the beginning, I went through and applied those prayers to every product that we made—past, present, and future.

Alice:
Scripted prayers like that have been an important part of my journey. I created a scripted prayer for when I work one-on-one with people for healing because I want to include everything that I love and make sure that all the pieces are there. God has done such amazing things through those scripted prayers.

Some of what I'm contending for is to create very big pieces. And then God flipped that and had me start doing these little watercolor sketches. I don't normally use watercolor; I do multimedia acrylic with a lot of layers and textures and various objects. This is the simplest form of my work ever. But I've started with each group of people: individuals, family, friends, communities, states, nations, and the world as well as divisions within each: body, mind, soul, heart, and spirit. I want to make sure that I'm covering all those areas. So I created the piece first, but then I wrote out a prayer to post on social media. I previously resisted writing out prayers because I didn't want to dictate to people how they should pray or how they should see my work. But I felt as if it were very important for these pieces. I'm rethinking my original stance on using scripted prayers because they've received a lot of positive feedback. (You can see those here: https://alicearlene.com/artful-prayers/)

With scripted prayers, you have somewhere to start. I'm not saying that's the only way for you to pray. But if you aren't confident in how to pray, then at least you can do this to start. God generally works through me more when I'm moving rather than when I'm sitting. If I'm just sitting, then I need to get moving, and then I move a little bit this way and a little bit that way. Here we go!

Once you've started using a scripted prayer, you will probably find that God adds to it, which will then build your confidence as you learn to pray with him.

I'm involved in another mentoring group, and the leader talks about God raising up an army of artists. I thought, *Well, it's time to fight.* I didn't start these watercolors based on a lovely thought. I thought, *All right, I am done with this negativity. I'm done with all this hatred. I am done.* I have friends and family and people from all different walks of life. And they're all great people. I was angry that people were talking badly about these friends, and these friends were talking badly about these other friends. So I decided to fight. And this is how. This is my war. And this is my weapon. It's a lot more militant in intent than how it comes across. I don't necessarily want the paintings to come across as a weapon, and I've been very intentional about the language so that they're not. We all want peace; we all want hope. We all want courage; we all want the wounds of our past to be healed. We can all agree on these points. So this art is militant with both a sword and a hug, you know?

Seneca:
Well, so much of the wounding is playing into all the drama today. In late 2020, I was fighting by including these little freebie products with orders. I was looking at what was (and still is) going on in the world. We were all collectively going through this crisis together even though we were having different experiences. But this was the only time when I felt as if everybody were dealing with some of the same struggles, so I could create very specific blends for people based on this.

In mid-December 2019, I had this really strong impression that I needed to sit down for thirty days and listen to God for a strategy for the next year. I did not know what was coming. But God was saying, "You need to listen to me!" So I actually made myself a blend for prophetic revelation and making the hearing process easier. Then I thought, Well, I should just take everybody with me. So I wrote out a thirty-day program that went with the blend and started people on it. I was basically teaching people in all walks of life in a secular setting how to hear God during that thirty days. And it was one of the most successful things that we've done. At the end of the thirty days, they had their own journal full of wisdom for the new year. That was priceless.

And I thought, *Well, this little freebie is going really well. Let's keep doing that.* And so we came out with this Bravely You blend and the thirty-day program, which was all about unmasking—taking off your metaphorical mask. We wrote this in February right before COVID blew up and masks became commonplace. I didn't have any idea that would happen. The next program we ran was called Adapt with a blend for adaptability. And that was in the throes of lockdown when people suddenly had to keep their kids home and figure out how to work their job or not work their job or whatever they were doing. Some were essential and had all these crazy new rules to follow that changed daily. The whole year, that's how it went. We would create a blend, then have a eureka moment of "Oh, here's why!"

So that's our goal for this book and class—for you to have similar experiences although they obviously won't be exactly the same because your business is different than ours. But God is so creative, he can do this in billions of different ways. How will you give your clients and customers a supernatural result that they can't get from the next business down the street?

CHAPTER 2

The Kingdom-First
Approach to Business

"**B**UT SEEK FIRST his kingdom and his righteousness, and all these things will be given to you as well" (Matthew 6:33). There are diverse interpretations as to what it means to "seek first the kingdom of God" as well as what the kingdom of God actually is. As business people, we have a unique role in expanding the kingdom on earth. We need to broaden our thinking of how we can bring heaven to earth through our business.

I reflect on Eden as our original outpost, that corner of the kingdom brought to earth, to be expanded upon until the whole world was colonized as the kingdom of God. We know how that went, and we are now in the do-over process, only with a lot more people and millennia of brokenness and destruction. We have work to do.

In John 18:36, Jesus said, "My kingdom is not of this world." He also said, "If I cast out demons with the finger of God, surely the kingdom of God has come upon you" (Luke 11:20 NKJV). If we need to understand what the kingdom is, we can look to the works of Jesus and heaven as our model of what should and should not be happening here.

So here we are, caught in this space between sacred and secular though that is a completely man-made construct. Our role doesn't change just because we go to work. But how we operate as a business should.

Earlier, Alice and I shared some examples of the kingdom of God breaking through in our businesses on our customers' behalf. What we'll do now is help you think about how the kingdom of God can be brought into this realm through the vehicle of your business and help you develop a plan to be more intentional about it.

We get stuck in the mode of praying for what we and our business needs, and everybody else is a second thought. But that's not actually how it's supposed to work. Every successful business, whether Christian or not, is based on serving others and meeting needs. The opening verse suggests that you put the kingdom first in order to get what you need. So how can you be intentional about that from here on out? What does the kingdom look like in your situation?

Secular sources offer this marketing advice: Find your niche, your audience, your ideal customer, or customer avatar. In other words, figure out who your product or service is for. What is your main demographic? They want you to find the person's so-called pain points or the problem they have and will pay money to resolve. If you've already done that, great. We will use that information but a bit differently than you've seen. We won't use that information to trigger them in order to sell the solution, or rub salt in their wounds so that they buy our product or service; we will use that as our marker so we can bring about a kingdom shift.

We can look at our products and services, what motivates people when they make a purchase, and how we can address the issue from a kingdom perspective. For example, my best-selling product is an anti-procrastination aid. People buy it once and buy it again and again because they want to accomplish more.

The easy way out is to pray for them to accomplish all that they set out to do. But is that really the highest and best?

Now, I'm not saying I know the highest and best, but I do know that empowering someone to run around like a chicken with their head cut off is not as great as motivating someone to discern the right things and do them at the right time in tune with flow. What I can do is pray over my products and the people who use them. I can pray for their discernment about projects and God-ideas so that they can get off the hamster wheel. Through prayer, I can release resources, blessings, and God's revelations to them. I can release forgiveness to them for times when they've shrunk back from their true calling, saying, "That's too much. I can't do it." This, in turn, releases them from the repercussions and vicious of that belief and frees them to see things differently. I can pray they now have courage to take on that thing. I can command their freedom from captivity and a release of their gifts, talents, generational blessings, and provision. And I can pray they have wisdom to instantly see how to defeat obstacles, know their purpose, and discard the busy work. I don't pray for individual people typically, but I can pray over a formula that's going out to hundreds or thousands. Tangible products can be a carrier, just like Paul's handkerchief was in Acts.

"IN JESUS'S NAME"

Let's address praying in Jesus's name since it goes along with what we're talking about in terms of a higher perspective when praying. John 14:13 says that whatever we ask in his name, he'll do. And we're all about asking big in this book.

People ask me all the time if I pray in Jesus's name. (I really scare a lot of people, so they have to ask.) My answer to that is probably just as off-putting. I say, "If you mean, do I tack 'In Jesus's name' onto the end of a prayer like an incantation, then no. If you mean do I operate in his nature—in his faith; his love for Father, us, and creation; his passion, compassion, and outward expressions that he has gifted us through the indwelling of Holy Spirit—then I certainly aspire to."

In Hebrew culture, "name" is synonymous with nature or character. That's why God changed the name of so many Old Testament people after they had an encounter with him. If you reduce praying in Jesus's name to the string of words that you tack on to the end of a prayer to make it work, then that is an incantation or witchcraft.

I imagine praying in Jesus's name to be a matter of having the mind of Christ, stepping into him, taking on his nature and character, and praying from that position. It's praying kingdom prayers. No wonder we get whatever we want when we ask in Jesus's name!

HOMEWORK:

For your first homework assignment, we have a worksheet with a couple of questions to help you implement this prayer objective. We've allowed some space to draft a big (big as in thinking big, not long and wordy) kingdom prayer. If you'd like a printable worksheet you can download, you can find that online in the class. SupernaturalBiz.com

Important! We've all been praying for our businesses. **This is not more of that.** This is to help you go after the kingdom on behalf of your customers and use your products and services as a vehicle to do just that. Please look at the example worksheet provided here.

You can list bullet points or completely script out your thoughts. You can think in terms of your overall business, choose a single product, or focus on your service. If you want to get gung ho and do a bunch of products, you can print out as many sheets as you need. I'm including a filled-in example using the product I was talking about above so you can see how it looks. Like I said in the video, I use bullet points and pray over every item of that product in existence and apply it to all future products. It's great to pray over additional batches, but I like an initial full-coverage prayer just in case.

Next, we'll talk about those other "things" referred to in our opening verse.

Kingdom First Worksheet

Example

1. Name of product or service:

   M&M flower essence

2. Who are the people that buy from you?

3. What's their main problem?

   Middle aged and older women who are deeply spiritual and like natural remedies. They have trouble getting everything on their to-do list done. I'm guessing there are a mix of things that they probably feel obligation on, things that are valid responsibilities, fear of hard things, lack of confidence at times, being swallowed up by other people's ideas of what they need to be doing. Need to discern and prioritize accordingly.

4. How can God pick up where your product or service leaves off?

   God can break through the mind clutter and help them choose the right activities, show them the difference between purpose and busy work. When they reorient toward their purpose, he can bless them in what they do.

Kingdom First Worksheet

1. Name of product or service:

2. Who are the people that buy from you?

3. What's their main problem?

4. How can God pick up where your product or service leaves off?

Kingdom First Prayer Template

Example

Things I'm asking God for:

    1. To tweak the formula to what each person needs to get stuff done

    2. Infuse His light, life love into each bottle, dunamis power that they would be excellent of soul.

    3. Show them purpose vs busy work or people pleasing

Things I'm releasing forgiveness to the client/customer for:

    1. Every time that they've said "I can't do this" and turned away from a calling or God-given assignment

Things I'm commanding to go or binding: (Warfare)

    1. Voices dissuading them

    2. All enemy intervention against their calling and assignments

Things I'm releasing or loosing: (Blessings)

    1. Kingdom building strategy to go with that new drive

    2. Their gifting, callings, resources, blessings and purposes from captivity

    3. Discernment for the right projects to work on

    4. Wisdom to get free of projects that are wrong for them

    5. Joy for the "doing"

    6. Grace for planning, organizing, delegating and multi-tasking

Kingdom First Prayer Template

Things I'm asking God for:

1.

2.

3.

4.

Things I'm releasing forgiveness to the client/customer for:

1.

2.

Things I'm commanding to go or binding: (Warfare)

1.

2.

3.

4.

Things I'm releasing or loosing: (Blessings)

1.

2.

3.

4.

CHAPTER 3

Vision before Provision

"**W**HERE THERE IS no vision, the people perish" (Proverbs 29:18 KJV). This is because provision only comes to support vision. A written, compelling vision is the foundation for this process. Everything we do for the future will build on this. This will get you out of bed in the morning, inspire you to follow through on your business homework, and get you focused in the right areas.

You need to put vision ahead of provision. So many people have this backward. They abandon dreams because they don't believe that opportunity, finances, time, etc. will manifest for them. Using lack as an excuse to build a wall to your vision stops here. A focus on provision usually results in a lack thereof; therefore, we are focusing up front on vision.

The word "provision" is made up of two parts: "pro" ("for" or "in favor of") and "vision," which signifies being able to see the end from the beginning. *Merriam-Webster's* actually defines vision as "unusual discernment or foresight."[1] So provision is what comes to you at the beginning for the purpose of taking you to the end goal. Vision must precede provision.

Provision can take many forms. It's usually thought of as money but can be any resource, skill, talent, connection, or opportunity that will get you to the end result.

The science behind this may have to do with your reticular activating system. Your reticular activating system acts as a filter between the conscious and subconscious minds. It lets you ignore background noise yet still notice when your name is being called. Its function is to get you to pay attention to what is important while filtering out all the ancillary matter.

For this reason, getting deeply in touch with your vision will program your reticular activating system to be on alert wherever you go and whatever you do. You can then take advantage of opportunities that will move you closer to your vision.

This is what it looks like in real life. My husband decided he wanted a Toyota Tacoma pickup with an extended cab. From then on, he saw these trucks everywhere and kept commenting on them. When we drove by a car lot, he would glimpse the roof of one way in the back that would be impossible for anyone else to pick out of the pack. "That's a nice little Tacoma," he'd observe. Anytime I went anywhere with him, we found trucks to test drive. Fortunately, he had also decided on some other specifics, including price and mileage, so it took him a while to find *the one*.

Dad was the same way about dead red fir trees. (We used wood heat.) He could drive down the road and somehow see one that nobody else saw. You had to hike back into the forest to reach it.

The goal for this week is to create your ideal written vision for not only your business but also for your life. Your business model will need to support or at least not hinder all that you are called to do, which will go beyond just business.

Almost all entrepreneurs sought to leave the rat race and have more freedom, flexibility, and time to spend with family or other pursuits. So they decided to start a business. But they usually end up working harder at a business than they did at their day job. What was intended to bring freedom became a prison. If you do this right by setting your priorities and needs up front, you can avoid or minimize the pitfalls. Many of you already have a business and may be dealing with feeling as if it is consuming all your time. While it's true there can be a lot of time-consuming upfront work, let's focus on where you want to be so that the transition can begin.

Business is often your means of being able to do what you need to do. Your calling in life may or may not have anything to do with business. Your business can provide the finances, and if you structure it right, it will provide you with a flexible lifestyle so that you can carry out all that you're called to do. Granted, God can work out the details if he wants us somewhere doing something, but we have a degree of responsibility to not get ourselves into bondage in the effort to make a living.

Your vision should be exciting and feel big and even intimidating and overwhelming. Be bold! Don't worry about the how. That will unfold. On a scale of one to ten of exciting possibilities, your vision needs to be a ten in order to captivate and motivate you and turn you into a magnet for provision. Reaching a ten may not be easy if you've made a life of putting everything and everyone else first. Keep working at it.

Have you ever wondered about Psalm 37:4–5 that tells you that God gives you the desires of your heart? Everybody gets all wound up about whether their desires are in line with what God wants for them. Mom made me learn Latin so I could take words apart and analyze their meanings. "De" is "from" or "of;" "sire," of course, means "father." *From Father.* Any questions?

What if it isn't just your flesh? "For it is God who is producing in you both the desire and the ability to do what pleases him" (Philippians 2:13 ISV). I love this verse. Read it again. "For it is God who is producing in you both the desire and ability to do what pleases Him." What a relief, right? Everything you need is already in you! What if all the stuff religion was trying to snuff out of you is actually what you're *supposed* to do?

I think I take it for granted that I work with delighted people. It might be worth examining your motives if you have any doubts. I don't question people's desires. Even those who insist a desire isn't godly probably are not looking at the essence of the desire but at its outward display. For instance, a person who wants to be a bank robber desires money, adrenaline, and risk, none of which are wrong. But robbing banks *is* wrong.

There's plenty to be said for knowing specifics, but you might first need to determine what you really want and detach from the form it might come in. For instance, you can have a set income in mind, but perhaps it's not really about the dollar figure but what that amount of money will provide. You might be able to engage with your vision much better if you realize you are pursuing financial security and plenty of relaxation and fun. That might take more or less money (income) than what you thought. The same goes with knowing specifics for a business. An understanding of the why behind the what can open the door to answers beyond what you could ask or dream. Note the specifics but include the motivation behind those. I wanted to be a florist, writer, and veterinarian as a kid. All of those desires are now intertwined in a creative business that is uniquely mine.

Big Visions and How Much You Think You Can Take On

I've been questioning whether I can and should be taking on this latest new project. I'm involved in a lot of different things, and I'm effective in multiple areas, but I'm always asking what is for now, what's for later, where does my focus need to be this minute, etc. I had a day plagued with doubting I can take on one more new thing. Then I had this dream.

SENECA'S DREAM

I was doing drugs and wanted to buy some speed, so I went upstairs to apartment 2 where my dealer lived. He hooked me up with the speed but also gave me birth control pills so that I wouldn't become pregnant while I was doing speed because he didn't think that would be good for me. But I did not think the birth control pills would be good for my body, so I refused them.

Interpretation: When we are experiencing anything negative, the second heaven will quickly cash in on our vulnerability by offering us an attractive option. In our moments of fear, doubt, pain, etc., the enemy offers coping strategies, and sometimes we end up making a short-team deal that is horrible in the long run. After all, I can cruise through all my current obligations much faster if I'm not conceiving and birthing new visions, innovations, and endeavors. But where's the future in that?

A subtle implication here is that I would not give the baby the appropriate attention, so it was better not to birth it at all. That may or may not be true. God knows what you're capable of. And he can bring the aid you need to pull it off. Conventional wisdom says that you can only do so much. I'm saying not to limit God, but pray, pray, pray about what's right for you. If he says, "Yes, you can," then who are you to argue?

Prayer to break agreements with the enemy regarding business and to release new concepts:
Lord, I repent of any deals or agreements I've made with the enemy when I've said I can't take on anything new. I refuse any of the enemy's attempts to abort or control me by preying on my doubt. I ask that I would be able to conceive in your timing, and I ask for the ability to recognize new opportunities and the faith and grace to carry to full-term what you desire to birth through me. I ask that I would always stand firm and discerning against that which would be destructive to those in the body of Christ under my care. Amen.

Fill out the worksheets as best as you can and post the answers below. You'll write out a vision for your overall life in a paragraph and engage with that *daily*. You will also write one for your business. This is the part where you daydream. Many of us haven't done that in years and will be rusty. This is not a once-and-done endeavor. I want you to be very intentional about setting aside time, at least twenty minutes, to do this *every day for a week*. (Don't worry if you go longer.) Give your imagination over to Holy Spirit and let him sharpen it and add to it. Make notes throughout the week as you go deeper, see new things, and get new ideas.

Sometimes, I think he is just waiting for us to figure out what we want and specifically voice it. Most of the time, we are not specific about what we want; we just know what we don't want. As I have looked over worksheets from previous classes, I am amazed to see that previous students have attained some and are close to other goals that they identified and wrote down. They can move forward.

This conversation between Alice and the Cheshire Cat illustrates what I'm referring to.

"Would you tell me, please, which way I ought to go from here?"

"That depends a good deal on where you want to get to," said the Cat.

"I don't much care where—" said Alice.

"Then it doesn't matter which way you go," said the Cat.[2]

We're all mad here. So that you don't cast me into the role of the Cheshire Cat, you'll need to spend some time soul searching and also invite God into your visioning process. You'll need personal revelation on the details. This is why Paul prayed that God would "give to you a spirit of wisdom and of revelation in the knowledge of Him … that the eyes of your heart may be enlightened, so that you will know what is the hope of His calling" (Ephesians 1:17 NASB).

You don't have to have all the right answers anyway. Your vision can take a lot of editing and expansion.

Before I cut you loose with your homework, Alice has a few tools to help you. Again, watching the video (SupernaturalBiz.com) might clarify what she's asking you to do.

Alice

People tend to encounter a lot of resistance in doing vision work because the enemy wants to keep you stuck. You'll never do what God gave you to do if you're stuck. I have a simple tool that I can teach you. It's called a collarbone statement. The collarbone point is the soft hollow just under your collarbones. It's a little bit tender, so don't press too hard. Just lightly rub it in a circle with your fingertips. You can then make a positive statement that you want to be your new normal.[3]

I have some statements prepared that I'll go over with you. So you're going to rub your collarbones. Then say something like, "I can dream with God. I can dream with God. I can dream with God."

Make your new statement (whatever it is) three times, then open the palm of your hand. Karate chop your fingertips with your other hand. We call it the karate chop point. That tells your system that you want it to accept this change. This is our new truth.

Other new vision statements might be, "I can see what God has for me to see." Or "I have complete hope because God is with me." This is a great time to personalize and apply some Scripture, and you have that double weightiness of the truth of the Word as well as working with your body's energetic system in order to shift your mindset. Given what we were just talking about in the video, another big one is "I already have resources that I can use." So you can customize this however you like, but it helps to decrease that resistance. That way, you can be at peace, be calm, and hear as clearly as possible from God. The possibilities are endless because we serve an endless and infinite God. There are no limits.

HOMEWORK

1. Fill out your vision questionnaires. Again, if you need to print one, you can go here: SupernaturalBiz.com. Do the lifestyle one first. Make it the absolute best it can be. Suspend all doubt, worry about obstacles, or fear about how you'll get there. We will be working on practical matters over the next few chapters, but that's not your focus right now.
2. Spend a few minutes each day this week engaging with your vision and imagine that it is already attained. If you continue to see it as off in the horizon, then it always will be. Pull it into your present. Daydream about what your life and business will look like. If you sense new positive details, add them to your written version.
3. Release your vision to God. Ask him to deal with any limited thinking or dreaming you have, and work on issues with Alice's healing tools.

Lifestyle Vision

If you had your ideal life, what would that look like?

Name 5 things you dream of having:

1.

2.

3.

4.

5.

Five things you want to be

1.

2.

3.

4.

5.

Five things you dream of doing:

1.

2.

3.

4.

5.

No judging! Don't put altruistic and self-less stuff down just because you think you should. This is an exercise in reversing repression. If you have trouble identifying what you want, consider what you hate and put down the opposite.

Business Vision

If you had your ideal business what would that look like? (Income, business structure, number of employees/consultants/partnerships?

How many days a week do you want to work?

How many weeks or months vacation do you want to take?

If you had no limits on time and money, what would you do/create?

If you had a magic wand?

What do you feel energy and excitement around?

CHAPTER 4

Your Comprehensive Marketing Plan

I F SELLING IS hard for you, then you need a paradigm shift.

Very few of us like wearing the salesperson hat. It conjures up all kinds of ideas about slimy tactics, manipulation, and other methods that people with consciences want no part of. Yet we still have to run our businesses. Most marketing is manipulation (witchcraft), so it's no wonder we, as Christians, are put off by it.

Even so, if your present view of sales and marketing is that it's a necessary evil, you're in danger of self-sabotage when it comes to promoting yourself and your product.

Like most concepts, there's a ditch on either side of the road. There's also a way to sell without being sleazy or annoying and without blackening your soul.

Your Offer to the World

It all starts here. You have to sell something you truly believe in and know that it's in people's best interest to buy from you. You can't only be in it for the money.

If you don't believe 100 percent in what you're doing, you shouldn't go any further in business until you address this issue. Do you simply struggle internally, or do you need to sell a different product or service? Do you need to improve or change your product or service or change your belief?

If you haven't already done so, I would urge you to write out a list of benefits that should form your sales copy. If you're dealing with self-doubt and limiting beliefs despite evidence to the contrary that your product is worthy, this list will help you get in touch with the value you give people.

The other side of this coin is giving your product or service away because you know how good it is and you just want people to benefit from it.

But if you really want to help people, you need to charge because people rarely value what they haven't paid for. You need to earn a living. Charging will also help you take your offer to a larger audience, which benefits even more people.

Sales Is Service

Shift your mindset so that you consider your job as a salesperson to be helping people identify what they want or need and how you can help them get there. Hopefully, that will be through your product, and if not, steer them to the right thing. Listen and be helpful first.

Sales Is Also Education

Like offering a service, you might need to spend some time educating people why what you have helps. Many times, they don't even recognize the source of their problem, let alone what they can do about it. Selling via education will be perceived as you doing them a favor if you do it right. Blogs, books, free e-courses, informative emails, and social media posts are all examples of this.

Sales Can Be Entertainment

We've all seen the funny commercials and have read entertaining sales copy. If you are a natural entertainer, let that be one of your sales methods.

Not Everyone Is Your Customer

I run a flower essence business. Do I believe everyone should use them? Of course! But I market to very specific types of people because I know who is interested and willing to work on their emotional issues. I spend my time and marketing budget there because I know I will never have to do a hard sell to those people. It's not my job to convince anybody to be my customer. My job is to help the people who are actively looking for a solution that I provide. Knowing your audience will save you a ton of frustration.

Shift your perception of sales away from the idea of trying to convince people to buy from you to helping as many people as you can. If you do that, you'll feel better about the process. As Zig Ziglar says, "Selling is not something you do to someone, it's something you do *for* someone."[4]

Let any of the above three—serving, educating, or entertaining—be a part of every interaction a prospect has with you, and you can't go wrong.

So let's get into some marketing. No matter what business you're in, people have to know, like, and trust you. If you are always looking for ways to establish those connections with your audience, you'll go far.

The Five Stages of Marketing Are as Follows

1. Attract prospects
2. Build relationships
3. Present the opportunity
4. Convert/sell
5. Retention and repeat business

This is more or less the journey people take with you, and more and more people tend to drop off with each level. You will need to nurture your people through this process to get them to take the next step with you. If you can effectively steward the clients and customers you have, you'll have a better business with less money and effort invested but a greater return on your money and investment.

If you spend all your efforts chasing down new customers without having a system in place, that is not effective marketing. However, most people do exactly that and focus intensely on stages one and four.

In this chapter, we will look at all of these stages and make sure we are effectively managing each. We'll look at various strategies for each stage and choose one or more that fit our businesses and line up with the vision, values, and natural propensities and gifts within us.

What we will not do is push ourselves in a direction we think we ought to go because it's popular and because other people are doing it successfully. Instead of trying to shore up our weaknesses and get better at those, we need to double down on our strengths and take those to a new level.

How Do You Communicate the Best?

All of marketing boils down to communication. It's really that simple. And to make it even easier, we want to look at when and how you are in the zone, so to speak, in your ability to communicate. I'm at my best when I'm writing. It's not that I can't communicate effectively through video (as seen in class), but if I really need to be specific and thorough, I will choose to write.

Other people might find the cursor blinking on the screen or the blank page intimidating and a long, hard process. But they can talk fluidly and coherently live and unrehearsed or with just a few notes.

Don't confuse your comfort zone with what you should be doing. Fear and resistance can often point to what you're meant to do, and the enemy might be trying to discourage you. A better marker of which methods you should use are what people seem to respond to the most and your natural strengths. If God put something in you, for heaven's sake, use it!

Establishing Credibility in Your Market

Many people have an internal battle over their credentials or lack thereof. They believe that they have to have a degree to be taken seriously or that they have to be already successful in a field. While certain fields require degrees or other sorts of paper credentials in order for you to legally operate, you can generally establish credibility in other less expensive, less time-consuming ways.

When an authority certifies you, you are usually obligated to operate according to their standards. This is to encourage uniformity and maintain their reputation. This is positive unless you have revelation to operate differently. You will have to step out from under that certification or else operate in rebellion. I now have certifications that I don't talk about.

There's also something to be said for searching out the matter rather than passively accepting what you've been taught, which results in greater ownership of your expertise. You'll be speaking from your own authority on the subject instead of parroting your teachers, perhaps without full understanding.

I believe God's intentions here are to take us all places beyond where others have gone before us. He wants us to travel along the waterways of the Spirit where we can flow without restriction from man's regulations and customs, so if you don't have the papers, don't write yourself off.

How to Prove Your Credibility without a Degree or Certification
- Your track record
- Your experience
- Social proof (testimonies, reviews, endorsements)
- Confidence
- Being direct
- Good grooming and dress
- Overall professionalism
- A dedicated website
- Your work in print (book, blog, articles, newsletter)

I use books to demonstrate my credibility for Freedom Flowers. These are some of my better sales tools. Amazon is its own search engine, full of people looking for solutions to their problems.

Imposter Syndrome

Who am I to talk to you about imposter syndrome? I mean, who do I think I am? It's not like I have overcome this and am some huge authority like Tony Robbins or something. Who in their right mind would even listen to me?

In case you didn't catch it, that last paragraph was an example of what imposter syndrome sounds like.

Imposter syndrome is actually a recognized issue in the secular world of entrepreneurs. We know it as the enemy yakking at us. I am actually glad that someone specially named this particular brand of accusation, so I'll use the term "imposter syndrome" from here on out. This is the voice that says that you're a fraud, you have no real authority in your line of business, and when you are found out, you'll be ruined, so don't act like you know anything *about anything!*

Hush.

It affects us all. If you think you can earn your way out of it, you'd be mistaken. As soon as you have the piece of credibility you thought you needed, it morphs into another accusing and demeaning thought. You might think it only affects people without the right education or experience, but that's not true. They have their own internal battles.

That doesn't mean you give up on seeking the right experience and education and work on leveling up in your skills, however. You do that because you are pursuing excellence, not because you'll finally feel as if you've arrived. If anything, more knowledge has the opposite effect—showing you how little you know.

But if you're waiting for this tipping point where you feel totally prepared and competent, you might never start a business or charge what you are worth, and you won't own your voice or fulfill your purpose. Beyond that, you're doing the world a massive disservice by not fully showing up.

In case you think this is humility, here's how you can tell the difference. Imposter syndrome will stop you from doing what you need to. It shuts you up—and down. Humility lets you show up and be imperfectly and transparently you, moving forward in your call. Humility comes with gratefulness for opportunities; imposter syndrome comes with feeling undeserving.

So suck it up, buttercup! You need to recognize where that voice is coming from and that it's an indicator that you are on the right track.

You also need to shift your focus from yourself and go help people in the way that you're called to. This redirect will immensely help you to bust past this negative mindset.

You may have heard the truism that God doesn't call the qualified; he qualifies the called.[5] Hang onto that one. We have a whole book filled with examples of people who did not initially look like all-star material. They stepped out in faith because they trusted God. We have the Bible. Secular entrepreneurs don't.

Imposter syndrome is most definitely a spiritual battle. (For more information on our spiritual battle, see Ephesians 6:10–18, 2 Corinthians 10:4–7, etc.) And by the way, business is most definitely ministry, assuming your motives are right. Imposter syndrome may have an intriguing name, but when you boil it down to the basics, it's the same ole tactics, so we can use our same ole weapons. Fire away.

STAGE 1 OF THE FIVE STAGES OF MARKETING

Stage 1 is attraction. It's how they first discover you exist. I'm sure you've already put a lot of thought into how you're going to put yourself out there. Let's focus on it some more. Here are some ideas.

Writing

You can tailor your writing for many audiences: a blog on your website, a guest blog on other people's websites with a similar niche audience, email marketing, articles for different publications, or a book that you market on Amazon with a strong incentive and instructions for taking the next step with you. Posting on relevant forums and social media to establish credibility counts as writing too.

Search Engine Optimization (SEO)

Search Engine Optimization (SEO) relates to where you show up and rank when people search for you on Google. If you don't rank highly, people will rarely find you in a search. Google is free traffic from people who are looking for what you offer and therefore not to be ignored. The best way you can be found in a search is by writing amazing, lengthy content. Not long ago, all the SEO hopefuls realized that Google wanted fresh content daily. They churned out a bunch of swill with the right keywords, of course, and ranked.

Now you can beat them with great in-depth articles that answer customer questions or solve problems. Google's job is not to get you indexed. Google wants to create the best search experience for the customer and bring up the most appropriate and helpful article. They will only improve these features in the future, so to take advantage of all these changes every time they introduce a new algorithm, just make sure everything you do benefits the customer.

If you are not a writer, keep in mind that YouTube is the second-largest search engine, and the first-largest, Google, loves to prioritize YouTube videos. Learning YouTube SEO is well worth your time if video is your strength. All of the algorithms side with the end user, though, so your best plan is to put the client or customer's needs first instead of taking the easy way out. The cream rises to the top.

Advertising

I have heard that advertising is not the best method for a service-based business as word of mouth is more effective. However, if you need to quickly get a lot of attention, I personally love pay-per-click ads and do well with them.

Networking

Networking is beneficial if your customers are businesses or business people. Otherwise, I'm skeptical of its effectiveness, but it is at least relational and can lead to joint ventures or partnerships between businesses that can help each other.

Joint Ventures

A joint venture (JV) is when two or more companies with similar audiences come up with a plan to work together to benefit each other's businesses. I'm already sorry for what I just said, but I don't want to be too specific and limit you as to how it's done. Odds are, you have seen a JV in action and not realized it. Ahem, this book and class.

I'm seeing a rash of business professionals who send out emails with this wording: "Hi Seneca, my friend so-and-so is having this free training on how to blah blah. He's a really great expert in this area, and I know you'll get a lot out of it. Here's my affiliate link because even though the training is free, my friend will upsell later, and I'll make lots of money if you buy." (The reason I'm seeing this so often is because it's working.) What better way than to have someone they already trust vouch for you?

I've also been seeing lots of bonus offers. Let's say I launch a class and am hustling to enroll people and you have a freebie that relates to my audience.

I can pitch my class, do a "But wait! There's more!" and add two or three bonuses that you and others fulfill. That might be your free introductory session, a workshop, an e-book, or something else that my people will love and get excited about and hopefully sign up with you as well as me.

Basically, JVs expose you to the right people that you would have a hard time reaching otherwise.

Fairs, Markets, and Shows

In-person events can effectively drive traffic to your product. If you can pull together a great-looking display, actively engage all day with those who attend, and create product or perform your service at the event, great! Have your newsletter sign-up information, a credit card reader, and free samples or information that they will actually want. It's a bonus if they will keep and refer back to it. Make sure to include your contact information.

Other Channels

Other channels are platforms like eBay, Etsy, Upwork, Udemy, Amazon, etc. The reason to sell there is because buyers are already there. The problem is that you have to deal with their terms and conditions. I have noticed a cycle with these kinds of platforms. They start out being a great option for sellers, and the policies shift to become less and less favorable. Never, ever base your entire business on one of these. Do not put all your eggs in somebody else's basket. Some of them? Definitely!

Many times, it pays to be an early adopter. Watch these platforms as they start. Not all make it, but if you can get a foothold in from the start, you can go to the top with them. The best time to start with Etsy was several years ago. For eBay, it was at least fifteen years ago. I'm not saying that your time

37

with any of these has come and gone, but it's more difficult to be successful on these platforms than it used to be. I'm even seeing that with Amazon's Kindle publishing.

Anywhere money is being made hand over fist, you can liken it to the gold rush. There will be crowds, exploitation, gaming the system, bad motives, and ultimately, a crackdown. You want to be there before all that hits and be well established in a position where nothing can touch you. To do that, you need to be in the right place at the right time, which probably means taking a risk on a new, up-and-coming platform. You also need to operate ethically and according to the rules.

More and more, we seem to be moving toward a system where the good guys win. Social media used to be the thing. Back in the day, your Facebook page could spam your fans' newsfeeds with your promotional junk all day long. Now if you want Facebook to show your content, you have to put out what people actually want to see. Lots of marketers are throwing tantrums right now over these and other changes, especially for Google search and Facebook. It's frustrating when you've learned how to work the system, then they change the rules.

However, this is hopefully a change in the right direction for marketing as a whole. It demands you treat people right and holds you to a higher standard. If you insist on considering only yourself, they insist on limiting your exposure. Doesn't that make you happy as a consumer?

Getting Referrals

Don't leave this up to the whim of the customer. Ask for referrals. And don't just ask your current clients but ask past clients as well as people who know you and know your character and strengths. To generate lots of referrals, provide exceptional customer experience, of course, and when asking for referrals, be clear on the kind of people you want referred to you. Tell them who your niche is by saying, "These are the kinds of people I feel I can help the most. Can you think of a few people who might fit those qualifications and tell them about me?"

Work the referral process into your system as part of your checklist. That way, you'll know that you asked each client for a referral. Come up with a reward system: a free _____, discount coupons, thank-you cards, or something else to make them feel appreciated when they send you a new customer or client. Have it ready so that it's easy for you. You might want to have a gift certificate or coupon that you give or send to every client so that they can pass it along. Ideally, you would have both a printed and an email version. This should be for a complimentary consultation or a product or service that will benefit them yet leave them wanting more. This makes it easy for the person to give out because they are actually doing their friends a favor. If you can't provide a free offer, give them a nice discount.

If you do a gift certificate referral, be upfront about what you're doing. If they appreciate you, they'll be happy to try to link you with friends that are solid prospects. Here's some sample text.

"Merry Christmas (first name)!

I wanted to thank you for being a great client, and I hope you're happy with all your _____. It's a great honor to be working with you.

I would love it if you could refer me to some friends that you think would appreciate what I do. To make that easy, I have a gift certificate for a free session you can pass along.

You can either email it or print it out and stick it in a Christmas card. Hopefully, that will help you spread a little Christmas cheer, and I can get some exposure for my business. Feel free to send as many emails or make as many copies as you need."

If a client is willing to email their contacts with your coupon, ask them to send a personalized email to each person rather than a mass mailing. Provide them with some text they can copy and paste to make it easy for them and ensure that your proposal is communicated well. They can tweak the text to fit their personality if they want.

Put an expiration date on the coupon so that people can't put off responding indefinitely. You can also give a different gift code for redemption that corresponds with each referrer for tracking purposes.

You'll notice that we essentially just got rid of some Christmas shopping for them. Who wouldn't want to give something like that? And once somebody tries your service, they recognize the value of it. This is much different than trying to recruit somebody to be your sales rep.

Incorporate whichever of the above strategies are the most effective for you.

STAGE 2: RELATIONSHIP BUILDING

Stage 2 is where the "know, like, and trust" factors have to happen. After they visit your website, connect with you for the first time, and respond to your call-to-action, what needs to happen next?

In a perfect world, they hand you money, right? If you're selling a low-cost product or service, you can probably make some sales right away. It really depends on your business. For the most part, we are all too skeptical and jaded. You can look at ads from the '50s and compare them with today's marketing and see the adjustments that advertisers have made.

Blogging is a great way to let a little more of your personality come through while increasing your SEO presence and providing value to potential customers.

Most email systems will let you set up an automatic RSS to an email feed. This means the minute you hit publish, it goes to your email provider and mails everyone on your list, segment, or group.

If you don't have a newsletter opt-in box on your website by now, stop everything and get it done. The only time it makes sense not to do this is if relationship is not a factor in your business and you don't plan on retaining customers. People are slipping through your fingers as we speak.

Follow through with integrity. If you said your newsletter will contain three tips each month, then give subscribers three tips each month. If you follow through on exactly what you say, you will stand out from 90 percent of marketers. If a potential client can't trust you to send out a newsletter or be on time for a phone appointment, why should they trust you when you say you can get them the results they are looking for?

Social Media

I would recommend not trying to be on every social media platform. It's a serious time investment. Choose either a platform that your audience likes or that you like personally. Conquer it. Then, if you want to branch out, fine. I have the largest following on Facebook since that's where I personally like to be. I've hired out Instagram to somebody who likes doing Instagram. What works on one network doesn't necessarily work on another, and if you are not willing to go to that site and engage, then don't even bother.

Some of what you share through media, newsletters, or other written content can and should be personal. Share stories from your own life that would help your audience. Let people in. Add photos, videos, and posts about your life.

Remember, you are still an expert and need to come across as one, so your personal posts will be sprinkled in with professional content instead of using your business page as your personal dumping grounds. There is a lot of power in vulnerability. Share your struggles and how you overcame or plan to overcome. I have a whole bunch of strangers rooting for me.

While that might make most of you nervous, it's a great opportunity to let them see that you're a real person, and you'll see who they are as well. People will probably want to stand back and watch you for a while before they buy. So what provisions will you make for them to do that?

Here are just a few ideas that might help you.
- Your own YouTube channel or podcast
- Write a blog or do a vlog
- Have an email list and send regular emails
- Social media
- Classes or workshops, especially if they are free or cheap
- Ask questions and find out what they need
- Contact management systems
- Free resources, such as events, downloads, and samples
- Success stories, including testimonies, case studies, and social proof
- Keeping your word
- Your own Facebook group
- In-person events and being active in the community

STAGES 3 AND 4

Stages 3 and 4 are opportunity and making the sale. They blend together a bit, so I'm going to lump them into one category.

Stage 3 can take a myriad of forms, depending on your business. How you present the opportunity for people to buy will probably require a lot of listening to the Spirit and trial and error. I can give you some ideas to start with.

The obvious place that this can happen is your website. However, this may or may not be the most effective way to maximize your opportunities. A strong conversion rate for a website is from 1 to 3 percent. (Hint—don't let this be your ceiling; mine is between 5 and 6 percent.) A decent conversion rate for a free introductory session, live event, or similar promotion is from 30 to 90 percent. Your website alone, especially in the beginning when you have little traffic, probably won't cut it.

Let me just say that I'm not diminishing the need for a web presence. Your website is a great way to sell in your sleep or when you're otherwise preoccupied. It demands very little from you, so building something that converts well and gets traffic is important.

In order to sell without the sleaze, two premises must be in order. I previously mentioned these but want to emphasize this point.

1. You have to fully believe that your product or service makes a positive difference.
2. You have to operate from the perspective that not everybody is meant to be your customer. You may be selling something that would benefit everybody on the planet, but that does not mean everybody needs to buy from you. Your job is not to convince anyone to be your customer. Your job is to help them identify what they want, then determine whether your product or service is the best means of reaching their goal. That will mean that sometimes, they need to go elsewhere.

Let's get back to the first point for a minute. Believe in your product. If you struggle with this, you have three options.

1. Go sell something else
2. Improve the product
3. Deal with your limiting beliefs

If you don't believe in what you're doing despite positive feedback and the proof of results, then you will sabotage yourself in the sales department. (This is yet another example of imposter syndrome rearing its ugly head.) In addition, prioritize getting testimonials and feedback. Read and reread those daily until they sink in.

The Presentation

You can offer your presentation in several ways: one on one, to a group, scheduled or spontaneous, or a free consultation. It can also be a sales page on your website. You should develop your presentation to provide lots of value for the recipient of your pitch. Respect their time and put something in it for them, regardless of whether they buy from you. It's a great way to establish the "know, like, and trust" factor.

Let's look at the effectiveness of a complimentary consultation in more detail. You need to advertise this on your website with an opt-in box at a minimum. It may even be your hook so that they sign up for your mailing list. Or you may make the offer a little later to those who have expressed enough interest to get on the mailing list. As I mentioned before, you might give current clients coupons to give their friends. (You don't only have to do this at Christmas.) You also might include appointment-booking software on your site to make this as easy as possible.

Coaches and those who offer similar services should not necessarily offer a sample session. This is more of an introduction to see if this relationship is the right fit. You'll want to articulate that up front in the appointment. When you are upfront about the process, the client will feel more at ease. You can use wording similar to the following: "I want to help you get a lot out of this conversation even if we don't wind up working together. If it seems like we're a good fit and I'm confident that I can help you, I'll invite you to become my client at the end of the conversation, and we can sort out the details then.

Does that work for you?" Make it clear that you *only* want to work with people you know you can help.

From there, go over what they want. Dig in and help them get clarity. Help them find their true motivation. Direct the focus to one main issue. You probably can't effectively discuss all their problems in one sitting. If you can help them have a breakthrough in one area, they'll be thrilled with the results (and with you).

Ask them to identify the obstacles they face in relation to this particular issue. Brainstorm strategies for overcoming with them. Make suggestions and refer them to helpful resources. If your product or service is what they need, say so. If not, refer them elsewhere. During this process, you'll also gain a feeling for how resistant they are to change. If they are dealing with a victim mentality or seem unwilling to move forward and if you are not confident you can address that, then this person will need a lot of your energy for little to no breakthrough.

Talk to them about how you plan to continue if they were client if the following happen:

- all goes well in the conversation
- you would like to work with them
- you feel that you can make a difference
- your personalities jive.

Focus on the benefits instead of the features. The benefits are your results, and features are the how. How is always an afterthought.

Flat out ask them to sign up with you. Don't beat around the bush. You're not being pushy here nor are you needy or manipulative. You have nothing to be ashamed of as you are just extending the invitation. The only reason you wouldn't do this is if you don't want to work with them. You don't have to accept everybody that comes along. If you sense trouble or feel as if they will be a drain, wish them well and move on to the next client.

In more of a product-based business or one with a low-cost service, I'm still in favor of this overall approach, but use a more hands-off version. This includes education. My goal for my website is to help them understand if essences will help with their problem. This generally means quickly deconstructing their beliefs that flower essences are herbal products, essential oils, or for physical healing. People who are looking for these things need to be rerouted to another company. Our Flowerbot Maisie takes the place of the free consultation to help them quickly locate a potentially helpful essence though it's not the same as a human helper. I write books about healing, but only one of them is actually about flower essences. The others lay out alternative ways to solve problems and mention flower essences as an option.

STAGE 5: CUSTOMER RETENTION AND REPEAT BUSINESS

I don't know about you, but repeat customers are my favorite customers. We've already been through the education process, they already love me, I already love them, and they're rounding up new people for me. So they're easy.

Let's deal with a possible objection to customer retention right now. I manage to keep selling to the same people over and over again. I have a product designed to permanently heal, and you don't need to use it for life, unlike many drugs. People will judge my retention rate in one of two ways. They will either say, "Wow! That must be awesome stuff if they keep coming back." Or they'll say, "She's not getting anything done if they're working with her for years." The people in the latter camp will be resistant to working for customer retention, thinking they need a one-time solution to do right by the customer. It's different for every business, but I bet you can find a way to continue to provide value to them so that they would be thrilled to stick with you.

In my own business, once they sense relief from whatever drove them to me in the first place, they continue to set the bar higher. We discuss secondary issues or how they can fine tune to achieve their goals. I can help with PTSD, or I can help with procrastination. It makes no difference to me. In the words of a customer, "I've grown so much, it's mind-boggling. It's just that I'm ready for more freedom, ready to make sure that I have plenty of whatever I might need, and ready to expand."

Always look for the next step people can take with you.

At the risk of making you really depressed, every solution comes with its own new problems. This means that you as the solution provider can stay in business selling to the same people if you plan accordingly. If you provide a product or service, what will the client logically need next? If you have tried to get through checkout at GoDaddy, you've seen this in action. When you buy a domain, they offer you hosting, security, a professional email, and other add-ons for your business.

Here are other options to consider for your clients:

- Show other possibilities beyond what they're currently working on.
- Take time for gratitude or prayer for—and possibly with—the customers you have.
- Identify new needs.
- Offer unexpected value.
- Celebrate their wins. (They don't always do it and might not even recognize a win. Help them be more cognizant of progress.)
- Create continuity programs.
- Follow up on how they are doing.
- Show appreciation in various ways, such as gifts, discounts, verbal expressions, or just sending a Christmas email.

- Stay relevant and at the front of their minds through the use of Stage 2 activities like email and social media.

And now it's Alice's turn to take out our head trash.

Alice:
This is another tool that works with your energy system. Remember, when I use the word energy, I mean actual, physical energy, not the woo-woo type of energy. Our systems function on various types of energy, and our systems carry and store our emotions as subtle energy similar to electricity. This Belief Reset Tool helps you release the negative emotional energy, thoughts, and beliefs that are held inside and replace it with positive emotional energy, thoughts, and beliefs. Unlike thinking of a specific statement as we did with the collarbone exercise, this time you can think in terms of a general concept. This works really well for more global activities, such as sales and marketing.

The basic process is to first release the negative, then input the positive.

To release the negative emotions, thoughts, and beliefs, tap while thinking about the negative:

You can do this exercise either as an energetic shift, spiritually through visualization, or a combination of both.

Think of your negative belief or traumatic event as being stored in various parts of your body. Start at your toes and pull out the negative belief or trauma and pull it up and out, moving up the body until it reaches your hands that you've stretched above your head.

You can visualize this, and then wrap up that negativity in a ball or box and give it to Jesus or place it at the foot of the cross or on the altar.

To partner with your energetic system, lightly drag your fingertips from your toes, up your midsection to the top of your head, and then reach up.

You can combine both if you choose. I'm in favor of utilizing as many senses or forms of healing as possible for maximum impact, but I've seen both used effectively on their own.

Once you've released the negative, reverse the process to input and fill up all those spaces with the positive. If you've given it to Jesus, ask him what he would like to give you in return, and picture that being poured into all areas previously filled with the negativity.

You can do this multiple times with the same issue, as well as a multitude of different issues.

Often, I've found that long embedded negative beliefs or traumatic experiences exist in layers, and require multiple repetitions to establish the truth deep within you. I think it's partly due to the many times you've come into agreement with that negative belief or trauma. Sometimes you can pull them out as a group, and sometimes you need to do them one at a time, or in smaller groups at a time.

You also have the habit of the negative belief or behavior pattern that you may need to overcome. Sometimes the healing shifts the behavior quickly, and sometimes it's a process. And, sometimes new issues arise that have been hiding under the ones on the surface. That's all normal.

Example: The belief I want to overcome is that marketing is manipulative and slimy and I'm no good at it.

I pull up that belief from my toes to the top of my head and out through the tips of my fingers and/or give it to Jesus

Then, I reverse the process receiving what Jesus has for me and/or thinking about how marketing is helping people find something that will help them. Marketing can be honest and authentic. I can learn to market my business well. I can be successful in marketing.

When I'm doing this, I like to set a timer because I lose track of time. You don't have to do it for sixty seconds on the dot. If you go a bit longer, that's okay. I recommend you use this powerful tool as often as you need to for whatever issues you are facing. It's not specific to marketing. You can use it throughout your life for any negativity that you're facing.

So with your strengths in mind and fears on a shelf, let's dive into your worksheets! This was a huge lesson, but the worksheet is simple. When you're done, you'll have a tailor-made marketing plan. The lines between stages blur quite a bit, and the same activity might apply to more than one stage. That makes it easier for you. We just want to make sure that all stages are covered.

HOMEWORK

1. Complete worksheets and decide on one strategy you will implement in your business for each stage.
2. Block out time on your calendar for future implementation. You may need to develop an ongoing schedule to regularly do certain activities. You might also set a reminder to look at this again in three or four months. You can evaluate how it's going and see what you need to change.

Your Comprehensive Marketing Plan

Review the section on establishing credibility. What factors can you use to demonstrate your credibility? What is a good credibility enhancer to work on?

A head trash issue I need to work on is

A collarbone statement I can use is

Review each stage in the text lesson and ask Holy Spirit to highlight the right strategies for your business. Choose at least one activity for each stage that seems right for you to take on.

Stage 1:

Stage 2:

Stage 3:

Stage 4:

Stage 5:

CHAPTER 4

Natural and Supernatural Time Management

W E'RE GOING TO go into some spiritual aspects and several practical points and try to make this as actionable as possible. As you read, write down some takeaway notes that seem like viable tweaks to the way you currently do things.

We live in a society where the prevailing belief system is one of scarcity, especially where time is concerned. But we need to get through our heads that this is false. We have enough time. *You have enough time to do absolutely everything you're called to do.* We get into trouble in the area of accepting false responsibilities. Other time wasters also distract and derail us.

This is why you must have a clear vision. If you do not have a clear and compelling reason to move forward, you are vulnerable to distraction. You'll wander in whatever direction the wind blows, following whatever seems like a great idea in the moment. Keep your eyes on the prize.

As I mentioned earlier, "Where there is no vision, the people are unrestrained" (Proverbs 29:18 NASB). Without vision, we lack purpose and direction, which leads to a loss of productivity. You may want to revisit your written vision periodically for a dose of clarity and to get re-enthused.

TIME WARPING

A few years ago, when I was trying to run two businesses, write books, and work a six-day-a-week job, I started having some breakthroughs with time. I was speaking in tongues a lot, and by a lot, I mean one to three hours a day.

At my job, you had to be at certain places at certain times and scan a barcode to prove it. But my scans were too close together. Once I drove all over the place within one minute. (The trip should have taken fifteen to twenty minutes.)

I was out walking one day when a guy came flying out of his house, yelling at me. "How are you faster than me when I'm faster than you?" I turned around, waiting for his explanation. He elaborated that I could be out for a casual stroll while he power walks or runs, yet I always beat him. I hadn't realized I was in a race. Situations like that make me a little nervous that I'm being noticed. Evidently, I don't look like the Flash since he was commenting on how slow I seem.

This differs from supernatural transport. In reference, Phillip was supernaturally transported from his city to speak to the eunuch. I don't believe I've ever had that happen, although I certainly want that. I don't think it's that because I'm cognizant of everywhere I go. I don't have the gaps in time that transporters have. I seriously think time changes for me. I think about Joshua telling the sun to stand still so the children of Israel could keep on fighting. Well, I was fighting. I was fighting for my businesses, my marriage, and my personal life, but I was at peace.

HOW TO BEND TIME

I can somewhat lean into bending time and do it on purpose, but I don't really have a formula to explain it. I will tell you my observations and theories below. I can say that you can't do it if you're in a hurry. You can't do it if you're in a rough place mentally or spiritually, and you can't do it with a scarcity mentality.

I believe that entering into rest is a huge factor in this. One day, I was coming home, absolutely confused and feeling as if I could no longer stomach normalcy. It seems to be a side effect of spiritual jet lag. I wasn't sure what to do, so I decided to download some teaching from Ian Clayton and listen to him for a bit. I had no idea what I'd encounter in his teaching, so I randomly picked one called Seat Of Rest. It explained so much of how I was feeling and how bending time works.

Here are some additional thoughts on time.

1. Pray in the Spirit

As I said earlier, I really believe praying in the Spirit is where it started for me. While I think it was more of a catalyst to put me in a proper mind frame than the actual activity itself, it did the job. I'm not going to tell you that you need to put in the same amount of time that I did because this is certainly not done by works. But two hours a day blew the lid off for me in several ways.

2. Mind frame

You can't step out of time in anything less than full peace. Being at rest even in the midst of activity is key. A scarcity mentality in the area of time will block you. So will offense or any other negative dwelling place.

3. No time excuses

"I don't have time" can no longer be a valid excuse. This doesn't mean you say yes to everything; it means you can't use it as your go-to excuse when you say no to someone. Instead, tell them that you have other priorities right now.

4. One with God

Get a revelation that you are one with a God who is outside time; therefore, you are outside time too. He's in you, and you're in him. Head knowledge doesn't cut it. Ask him to personally reveal this to you.

5. Ask to walk in wisdom

I have been meditating on the following verse for a couple of years. "Walk in wisdom towards those outside, redeeming the time" (Colossians 4:5 LSV). It continues, "Your word always being seasoned with salt in grace—to know how it is necessary for you to answer each one." Ephesians 5:16 tells us "Redeeming the time, because the days are evil." That chapter is all about having your act together on an inner level and walking in wisdom. I'd recommend a review of that whole chapter since it does address being filled with the Spirit and speaking and singing in tongues.

If you're going to redeem time, wisdom is the common denominator. Wisdom, we are told, is available to anyone who asks. (See James 1:5.)

KAIROS VERSUS CHRONOS

Redeem means to take the power from another. *Chronos* is the Greek god of time. This is where we get the term "Father Time" and chronological time. We need to stop empowering that dude. Just so we're clear, other gods are demons. *Kairos*, of course, in the New Testament, is an appointed time in the purpose of God.

Wikipedia says kairos "signifies a time lapse, a moment of indeterminate time in which everything happens."[6] I quite like that definition. Kairos is smack dab in the middle of where we want to be. Redeeming the time, I believe, is stepping out of chronological time and into kairos.

Note: I don't believe that chronological time in and of itself is evil, only that we aren't to be subject to it. God uses it, and so should we. It should serve us, not the other way around.

We can't talk about time without bringing up some Einstein. He, of course, said that time is relative. "The distinction of past, present and future is a stubbornly persistent illusion."[7] Take that, chronos. We are made to have eternity in our hearts.

If you're in him and he's in you, then you're outside time. Actually, it's a dual construct, according to what you choose to engage. When you prophesy, you are pulling from the future. When you observe something in the past, you change it. Google the observer effect in quantum physics. You are always moving in and out of chronos time.

God uses chronos time because it helps us engage and savor moments. Otherwise, everything would happen all at once. But we are not meant to be limited or controlled by chronos time.

TIME CHANGE IS LINKED TO THE BATTLE BETWEEN GOOD AND EVIL

Time changed at the fall in Eden, again in the days of Noah, then again at the cross where the curse became null and void. This verse from Daniel's end-time vision is interesting. "And he shall speak great words against the most High, and shall wear out the saints of the most High, and think to change times and laws: and they shall be given into his hand until a time and times and the dividing of time" (Daniel 7:25 KJV).

Wearing out the saints gives validity to my view that a posture of rest is crucial. It's yet another kingdom paradox: To go faster, you get out of your hurry and rest. To be clear, rest in this case does not mean inactivity, rather finding your rhythm and being at peace in your work. As Solomon said, "I have seen everything that is done under the sun, and behold, all is vanity and a striving after wind" (Ecclesiastes 1:14 ESV).

What if "under the sun" meant under the sun's rulership? I had a dream where I was watching a documentary about Ra (the Egyptian sun god[8]) the other night. Solomon supposedly wrote Ecclesiastes late in life after he had been led away to follow other gods. He has written quite a bit beyond what Bible readers know. He has given the occult world some pretty juicy, trouble-making writings. All of that wisdom was channeled another direction for a while.

At one point, I found it useful to draft a prayer for myself. I tend to think better on paper, and I'm not a verbal processor whatsoever. Here's mine to borrow.

> I repent of any areas where I have not been walking in wisdom. I forgive those who have been careless with anyone's time—mine, theirs, and those that I care about. I ask forgiveness for judgments about time—mine and theirs. I repent for wasting time, not understanding time, or my relationship with it. I repent for every time I have used it as an excuse or believed that I didn't have enough. I repent for coming into agreement with chronos

and toiling under the sun. Any place where the sun, moon, and stars or seasons have had a right to speak into my life, I declare that the blood of Jesus speaks louder. I declare that I am free from their influence! Show me a better way! I repent of clock watching and schedule sticking. I declare those things serve me rather than me serving them. I am not a victim of a twenty-four-hour day.

I want unlimited time, not just in business but in relationships, at home, and in the garden (secret place). I want enough to go around. I ask for a repayment of time that's been lost, that the time would be supernaturally made up.

No longer will I run out of time; I declare that I am one with a God who is outside of time and space—therefore, I am too. I am not under the sun but the Son. I have all the time I need. Show me what to do with my time and teach me to steward it well. But also set my mind at ease so that I'm not worried about doing the wrong thing with my gift of time. I repent for thinking that I have to do big things with the surplus. And may there always be a surplus. In Jesus's name. Amen.

SOME PRACTICAL STUFF

The 80/20 Rule

This rule that experts apply to everything says that 80 percent of your results come from 20 percent of your actions. The problem is that most people spend 80 percent of their time on activities that get them 20 percent of their results. If you can identify and prioritize those 20 percent of the actions you take, you will get better results faster.

If you've ever seen one of those grids adapted from The *7 Habits of Highly Effective People*[9], daily time suckers are separated into four quadrants.

1. Urgent and important

2. Not urgent but important

3. Urgent and not important

4. Not urgent and not important

	Urgent	**Not Urgent**
Important	Crises Deadlines Medical Emergencies **1**	Planning Continuous Improvement Professional Development Marketing Proactive Actions to reduce quandrant 1 Creative Work **2**
Not Important	**3** Many Interuptions Some Emails Pressing Matters with Little Impact	**4** Facebook Most Videos Most Email Web Surfing Perfectionism TV

Most people spend their time working on tasks from sections 1, 3, and 4 and neglecting section 2. This set up a reactionary lifestyle so that you are spinning your tires. You're very busy but not getting anywhere. You need to make a deliberate effort to schedule your section 2 activities, which will produce 80 percent of your results. When you spend time doing those things in section 2, you have fewer issues and fewer fires to put out. Life flows along more smoothly.

You can accomplish more when you figure out how you instinctively function. The Kolbe A will help you do just that. It differs from personality or IQ testing. It tells you how to play to your strengths and what situations to stay away from. Another great test is the Marketing DNA test by Perry Marshall. While its selling point is marketing, it's really about making sure you're not wasting time and energy doing the wrong kinds of activities for who you are. You can buy it on his website, but if you buy the 80/20 book on Kindle, it's free.

LISTS

"I don't know how I get stuff done. I just wing it and hope for the best," said no productive person ever. You need to write down tasks.

But here's the problem with to-do lists. You have way too much crap on them to finish in a day, they list projects instead of tasks, and you're not prioritizing correctly. You do need a to-do list though, and you need to add to it as you think of new items. Keeping it all in your head won't work because you only have so much RAM, and you will come up with something random to accomplish rather than what really needs to occupy that time slot. I use todoist.com because the one thing I can manage to keep track of is my phone and the app syncs with my computer, tablet, and email. Oh, and it's free. It's also a list app that lets you add a project, group tasks under it, and assign priority levels and due dates. Five minutes of planning what you need to do tomorrow at the end of your day allows a clear mind and closure for the day. It also means that when you have a few minutes free, you have some jobs to fill that slot at your fingertips. You're welcome to use pen and paper, but if you don't have it with you everywhere you go, it's not effective.

You can have a massive to-do list, but you need to divide it into what you can handle in one day. I suggest picking from one to three things each day that are not urgent but important, depending, of course, on how much time each one will take. (I am not saying that you should only do one to three things per day but that you prioritize important but not urgent tasks rather than making a practice of only treading water.)

PROJECTS VERSUS TASKS

Think about this; if you had a list with several items on it like

- mail thank-you cards,
- publish e-book,
- schedule Facebook posts, and
- spell check blog post,

what will not get done is "publish e-book." That would have been the most important job that would move your career forward, yet it would have been the dreaded last activity. If you had listed an actionable task that is the next logical step of that project, such as "set up an account with Draft2Digital," you'd be on your way already.

Don't put projects on your lists. Break them down into actionable steps.

OTHER PRACTICAL IDEAS

Establish a morning routine. The first sixty to ninety minutes of your day should vary very little. If you're at it early, you can accomplish a lot before other people wake up and start throwing wild cards and pseudo emergencies into your day.

Work with your natural rhythms. What time of day are you the most physically energetic? What time are you most intuitive? When are you a deep thinker or more creative? Structure your day's activities around these cycles.

If you get tired, rest or shift what you're doing. I frequently rest by changing activities. It's as much energy management as it is time management.

On a perfect day, I can finish everything by noon and knock off. After that, I can give myself tasks that a trained monkey could do, but I am really better off socializing, napping, or reading. After dinner, I start to ramp back up and focus on writing, dream work, and the prophetic.

I also tend to group right- and left-brain activities because I recognize it takes time for me to shift between the two. I cannot write code for a website and then effectively minister on a prophetic team without losing time when I shift. But I can code in the morning and do other tech or financial stuff, then run some errands to get into my happy middle of using both sides of my brain, and later go hard to the right.

Practice basic self-care. Sleep if you're tired, eat when you're hungry, go to bed at a decent time, and feed yourself properly. If your work is physical, get some rest. If your work is sedentary, get some exercise. Set phone reminders if you have to. I don't have a wake-up alarm; I have a bedtime alarm. This tells me to power down, get into my jammies, wash my face, brush my teeth, and quit for the night. No more looking at screens. Otherwise, I'll work too late and sleep poorly. Alarms in the morning mean no dream recall.

Working on your Sabbath is counterproductive. This is one type of rest many of us have to labor to enter into. It's not as easy as it sounds to set aside all obligations. It involves trust that as you keep a Sabbath, you won't fall behind, and responsibilities will be taken care of. By the way, I refer to this as a "crash day" because the word "Sabbath" has a connotation of church, eating out, and anything but rest. I suggest that if you go to church, you pick a different day to allocate as a crash day. This takes some preplanning. You might need to gather twice as much proverbial manna the day before to ensure that you have a nice down day. Not working on the Sabbath might be the only thing I am legalistic about.

WHAT'S DRIVING YOU?

I got some strategy for this in a dream. I was supposed to do vehicle inspections to make sure you didn't have boa constrictors functioning as backseat drivers and that you had lights and could see out the windshield.

I believe this is very related to time management because if we are in need of better time management, it may be for the wrong reasons. You see, your forward vision—not what creeps up and squeezes the life out of you—is supposed to propel you. Be driven by excitement and passion, not pressure. This is why it's so vital to do your vision homework.

Make a list of things that suck your time and energy. What would you consider letting go of or delegating? Are you doing things that aren't in line with either your lifestyle or your business vision? What is the motivation behind these actions? Are you making somebody else happy at your expense? The best way you can serve others is to fully step into your calling. That won't happen if you make umpteen batches of cupcakes for the bake sale.

No is a magic word and creates all kinds of freedom. How you say no matters. Your subconscious hears what comes out of your mouth. If you feel the need to explain your no with "I don't have time," you're feeding yourself the same line of crap that you're telling them. Every time you say yes to an activity, consider what you are saying no to by doing so. Are you okay with that?

REASONS FOR OVERWHELM

Overwhelm attacks us for many reasons, including the following:

- Underestimating how much time activities will take and taking on too much
- Conversely, seeing a mountain that's really more of a molehill if you'd just get going
- Neglecting to implement a plan to reach objectives, which leads to less confidence
- Not physically or electronically recording everything you need to do into a system to remind you but keeping it in your head and mentally going over it.
- Lack of focus
- Failure to clarify priorities
- Perfectionism or taking too much time to do something right when good enough will work

When You Start to Feel Overwhelmed, Do the Following
- Reevaluate what is most important
- Make a list
- Break down the list into baby steps
- Take action immediately.

TIMED ACTION

For overwhelming, unfun tasks, I make a deal with myself and set time limits. I will only work on that task for X amount of time. The amount of time needs to be shorter than you think you can accomplish anything significant in, such as ten to thirty minutes. "I will only clean the kitchen for fifteen minutes."

Then I set a timer and go. (If a kitchen timer isn't handy, just use your smart-phone. "Okay, Google. Set timer for fifteen minutes.") When the timer goes off, you stop. That's important. Many other gurus tell you to do this and say you'll probably feel good enough to keep going. Nope. Do not sucker yourself into spending more time on that task. Keep your word. "I am only going to pre-schedule Facebook posts for twenty minutes." You'll be more willing to get started when there's a definite end in sight.

You might not be done when the time's up, but you'll feel better, and knowing you have a short time to work will keep you super focused on the job. You'll see what you're capable of when you set a firm intention, and you'll learn to gauge time better.

PREDETERMINE THE WORTH

Many times, I will predetermine the worth of a project. "_____ is only worth an hour of my time. If I can't get this done in an hour, this is not a good use of my time." I will then go on to something worthwhile. If I think I can do it in the amount of time I assign to it, I go for it and do the best job I can in that amount of time. Done is better than perfect in most cases. How many things have you put way too much time into when they end up being of little importance?

You just shouldn't be doing some things. There are ten-dollar-an-hour jobs and one-hundred-dollar-an-hour jobs. You do what brings in major revenue that only you can do and hire out some of the other work. This might not be possible in the beginning, but as soon as you can, start looking for what you can hand off to someone cheaply. You can outsource many online projects to India or Africa, pay less to accomplish these tasks, and help someone who really needs to make a living.

I have learned that you can't wait until you're drowning to hire help. If you do, you'll still be drowning, and you'll have to train people on top of everything else.

In the class video, Alice and I discuss working with planners and goal setting.

Alice:

I have purchased calendars and all kinds of organizational stuff over the years, and nothing ever seemed to work well for me. I would become very distracted. I used what I bought; then it wasn't working very well, so I wouldn't use anything, which was not successful. With my background in science, I love graph paper. So I started again with graph paper and created a modified bullet journal where I just wrote the month. I used weekly pages to write down my appointments. I had a lot of room underneath each weekly section, and I kept tweaking it over the years. I would draw the lines for each month as I got to it. I started refining what worked well for me, and I found I liked having a lot of room in the back where I could make lists and take notes for classes. I had different charts, and I kept track of what I was working on. I always had a section in the back for dates for the following year. Eventually, I finally figured out that this was really working well for me.

Next, I added quarterly goals. I break up the year into four quarters, then set goals for two or three large target projects. I assign one particular project to a week or two weeks or however long I think I need to work on it. For efficiency's sake more than anything, I now have these printed by Amazon. You can purchase them if you want, but I mainly did that just so I didn't have to draw the lines every month. This planner has an annual overview, a quarterly goals page, and a space for notes.

Each month I have a full spread so I have an overview of when I need to do what. That way, I can keep track of all aspects of my life because if I don't have everything in one place, I tend to forget that time is not necessarily flexible enough to allow me to be in three places at once. I have a weekly page where I keep all the details, and I still have space in the back of the planner to keep track of goals that I've achieved or what I'm doing. When I was doing my series of fourteen books, I used one of those pages to track where I was uploading each book and everything I needed to do for each one. I then checked each one off and kept myself organized as far as what I was doing for that massive fourteen-month project.

By submitting my desire to reach my goals to God but yet needing flexibility, he really worked with me to develop something that works very well for me and has enabled me to achieve what seems kind of crazy if you just say it. Writing fourteen books in a little over a year? That's a little ridiculous. But my flexible structure helped me reach that goal.

Seneca:
Sometimes we find the most freedom in a little bit of structure. You know, we don't want to go overboard in life. But some structure is good.

Alice:
Yeah, I don't function well with really tight structure although I tried and tried. I told myself from ten o'clock to noon, I'm going to do X. But that never lasted long. I would chuck it out the door. It's been much more effective to know which project is next and build in a cushion of time because life happens. That way, the unexpected doesn't derail the whole project. Breaking up projects by quarters versus the whole year helps me to reassess and refocus four times a year instead of just in January like I used to. We all know how well that usually goes.

HOMEWORK

Spend time in prayer even if you need to do other things at the same time. Build prayer into your lifestyle even if you don't set aside a specific time for it. Prayer brings about that peace that helps you transcend your situation.

Complete the 80/20 worksheet to determine your high-priority actions. This will be a bit of guesswork, prayer, and trial and error, but the goal is to start thinking in this direction out of habit from now on. Use a system for a to-do list whether it's on paper or the via the todoist or another app. Close out your day by scheduling from one to three important tasks for tomorrow. Spend time weekly planning goals and projects and breaking down the projects into tasks. Hint: You'll probably need to schedule this via a phone reminder so you remember to do it.

Start a list of what you need to do later. You need a place to keep all your ideas that belong on the back burner, a place besides your head. I have a "not doing now" folder in my email and a document list. These need to be periodically reviewed to be effective.

Check yourself throughout the day. Ask, "Am I being productive or just busy?"

Document what strategies you plan to implement this week to improve your time management.

OPTIONAL HOMEWORK:

Here's an optional mp3 that I have listened to over and over again: Ian Clayton's Seat of Rest mp3. Let's just say that if you submit to lordship, focus on what you're supposed to be doing, and are in a God who exists outside time and space, all of heaven and earth will conspire to move you forward.

Ian is not a preacher; he is a businessman who runs several companies. Yet he takes half the year off to travel and speak. This is where we need to be.

HEAD TRASH REMOVAL (ALICE)

Head trash can stop you from setting and achieving your goals and the activities needed to reach those goals. Self-limiting beliefs sabotage you and reinforce themselves with that failure. It's time to stop that!

When you make your action list on the 80/20 worksheet, make a note of the actions—or even of the bigger goals—that you feel negatively toward or that you seem to resist. Maybe you even resist writing them down at all. Sometimes that feeling and/or resistance is because others have set the goals for us, or they are things we feel we should be doing.

Don't should on yourself.

Maybe you don't need to worry about these goals right now or ever. This is a great time to work through the Head Trash worksheet and gain some clarity. Will these goals honestly help you get where God wants you to go? That hesitation could be God's way of telling you "not now."

If it's because you feel unworthy or not capable or other negative feelings, you need to deal with that. But it can be difficult to sort out your feelings if the fears are yelling at you too strongly. Work through the healing strategies I've taught you or apply any other tools you've used in the past that work well so you can gain the clarity you need to make the right choice for where you are right now.

In my artwork, I've been pushing myself to paint on bigger boards. When I outgrew my old set up, I needed to build a wall easel to handle the larger boards. I just froze. I kept making excuses as to why I wasn't going in there and doing that simple task. I'm in a few accountability groups, and after a while, it hit me that my reasons (read: excuses) weren't really valid, and I needed to sit myself down and get to the bottom of the resistance. Mine was a fear of success, and I'm still working through some of that. But once I identified it, I was able to get in there, build the easel, and prep the board.

And it didn't take near the time I thought it would.

Resistance often distorts the time something will take you so that you are tempted to quit and give up before you even start. And maybe it's a device of the enemy to keep you from entering into rest and experiencing all the effects that entails. The time will pass anyway, so you might as well get going on what matters to you.

After you've dealt with the resistance, do a gross estimation of how much time you think it will take. If you're good at this, the next step is easier, but I'm not, so don't worry if you have no idea.

As I previously mentioned, I plan my goals by quarters, which are thirteen weeks long. I choose three or four goals, depending on how much I have to do in each quarter. I keep all the goals and actions on a list at the front of my planner for future reference. I then assign the goals to weeks with the subset of action steps under them. I'll assign these according to how long I think they'll take.

I always leave one or two weeks free. I'll err by adding more free weeks, not fewer. This allows me to adjust my schedule if I need to or if an action takes longer than I thought it would. I have already built in a cushion of time to accommodate those changes without getting off track for the quarter. If an action takes less time, I'll backfill with another action from my list.

I still don't always finish my goals. So I'll carry over actions into the next quarter and use my increased knowledge and experience to adjust how long I think it will take.

This system is a tool. It is not cast in concrete. If I need to adjust my time because of illness or an unexpected turn of events, I'll reassess as needed.

Because I have several businesses that fluctuate as to how much time they take weekly, I don't always know how much time I'll have each week, so this adds to the complexity of scheduling. Before God helped me work out this system, I was easily frustrated and spent a lot of time trying to figure out what I should be doing.

By having a specific project for the week rather than for a day, I know what to do when I have free time in my work schedule. And because I recently worked on that activity, it's fresh in my mind, so I can pick right up where I left off. Often, my subconscious has been working on the project while I was busy with other tasks, and it flows really well. So if I think something will take two weeks, I typically schedule those back-to-back to take advantage of the fact that I won't need to figure out what I was doing before I continue.

I've given you two other handouts that you can use for this process. Assign the time by weeks or days or however you will most effectively plug those tasks into your schedule. I work out my weekly projects on separate paper from my planner so I can start over if I need to. When I'm done, I typically write the project on the Sundays for that quarter. That's my day of rest, so I don't have activities written on that day. I attend church every week, so I don't write it down.

The other important point in successful goal achievement is to celebrate all your successes. Determine a reward proportional to the difficulty of the goal/action and follow through when you achieve it. In addition to completion, consider the time spent working toward the goal if you're having difficulty getting started.

You see what you're looking at and for, so if you're looking for failure, you'll see it. But if you're looking for success, you'll see it, which highly motivates most people. Positive reinforcements are much more motivating than negative ones.

For example, if your goal is to exercise five times a week, and you're currently not exercising at all, then every day you exercise is one more day than you exercised before, right? Celebrate that even if you only exercise once a week. If you do, then once will become twice, etc. If you beat yourself up over not exercising more, you probably won't try again.

This is also a great reason to gather supportive people around you. They can celebrate with you and help you overcome resistance so you can achieve all your God dreams.

80/20 for Productivity

1. Choose a goal you want to accomplish

2. Brainstorm a list of all the potential actions you could take that might lead to you achieving this goas. Include any actions you're already doing as well as new ones. This is not the time for censorship.

3. Now the question to ask is: If I took 20% of these actions, which ones will get me the 80% results? Circle the top 20% category actions. (If you wrote 15, choose 3.) You are free to speculate here and give your best guess. Often we don't know until we try, but the more you engage this process, the better you'll get at determining which actions are going to be the most beneficial.

4. Work your circled items into your to do list. Don't take action on any 80% stuff until your 20%'s are complete. By then you probably won't have to do them.

Action Plans

Action Step	Estimated Time Needed	Target Time to Complete

Take out Your Head Trash about Goals

Conquer any Negativity

Are there any of the goals and actions you've done in the 80/20 exercise that you don't believe you can do? Or you aren't worthy of doing or having? Write out the action and that belief.

Write out the flip side of that - the positive and Godly statement or belief that you want to believe.

Use the collarbone statement (day 2) or release negative thoughts and beliefs (day 3) tools to reset your system for success.

CHAPTER 5

Keep Going!

NOW WE WILL look at the long term of how to continue forward long after this challenge. A hard stretch passes between the conception of a new business and actually having it made. During that time, you may or may not have quit working for the man, but now you will need to develop some self-bossing skills as well as implementing backup structure and accountability.

"The truly free individual is free only to the extent of his own self-mastery. Those who will not govern themselves are condemned to find masters to govern them. -Socrates."[10]

YOU DA MAN!

You either have already or are in the process of transitioning from working for the man to being the man. This is really simple. You already know how to do it. It is not, however, easy.

If you've ever held down a real job before, you have these essential skills.

1. You show up every day. In a job, that is what you do. It might be only to keep from getting fired, but you do it.
2. You show up, no matter what. You go to work when you're sick if there's nobody else or you can't afford the time off. You work when it's sunny outside, when your favorite TV marathon is on, and when your friends are all getting together for coffee and inviting you.
3. You stay there all day. You fulfill your responsibilities. You might slack, but you manage to do a good-enough job and provide enough value to the company that they keep you. You don't go home until it's time to punch out.
4. You accept payment for your efforts. In fact, you fully expect it, and the more, the better.
5. You don't take on your job as your identity. You might take pride in your work, but you don't let it define who you are. You can gracefully accept praise or criticism. You shift gears quickly from work to other aspects of your life.

Now, in contrast, the entrepreneur who doesn't self-boss doesn't show up every day. He certainly doesn't show up every day, no matter what. (Please note I'm not saying you can't have time off. I'm saying be structured and have a plan.) He comes and goes when he feels like it and as the wind blows.

He overidentifies with what he's doing and therefore may not be able to put a price on his services or accept criticism. As a result, he may not ever be willing to put out his work in public, or he does so in very safe ways, which translates to no publicity.

Here are a few Proverbs for you, just in case you thought you might be in danger of working your butt off without seeing a return.

- 22:29—"Do you see someone skilled in their work? They will serve before kings; they will not serve before officials of low rank."
- 12:24—"Diligent hands will rule, but laziness ends in forced labor."
- 21:5—"The plans of the diligent lead to profit as surely as haste leads to poverty." (Will you take shortcuts? Or will you be diligent and do the job right?)
- 10:4—"Lazy hands make for poverty, but diligent hands bring wealth."
- 13:4—"A sluggard's appetite is never filled, but the desires of the diligent are fully satisfied."
- 6:6–11—"Go to the ant, you sluggard; consider its ways and be wise! It has no commander, no overseer or ruler, yet it stores its provisions in summer and gathers its food at harvest. How long will you lie there, you sluggard? When will you get up from your sleep? A little sleep, a little slumber, a little folding of the hands to rest—and poverty will come on you like a thief and scarcity like an armed man."

This is what is in front of you for a while. Mastering self-mastery. But this isn't the goal. The goal is to have a business that sustains without you as a grunt worker. This is when you truly are "da man."

HAVE BACKUP

Different personalities need different types of support structures, which is a key to success that most people neglect. Without a plan in place, it's easy to get sidetracked and derailed.

Inspiration is a great motivator, but when the going gets tough and you've become negative, you need a back-up plan to keep you going.

Depending on who you are, your weaknesses, your preferences, your strengths, etc., you'll need one or more of the following: role models, mentors, coaches, accountability partners, mastermind groups, goal tracking sheets, reminders, scheduled review and planning times, etc.

When you have reinforcements in place, you'll be more strategic, inspired, and focused and better able to break through resistance.

We've talked about goal setting and time management. Again, my favorite reminder tools are todoist and the calendar on my phone. If you schedule an activity months in advance, you'll need a tool that puts it in front of your face at the right time.

A recurring noisy reminder that grabs your attention is a great way to start a new habit. You need to set it for about a month, and after that, you should be settled in a new habit.

I'm going to throw more ideas out there to ensure a successful structure. You do not need to do all or even half of them. You need to do what makes sense for you. Generally, you should focus on implementing one thing at a time. You might make a short list of success structures that you think would benefit you. Start with one. Put in a reminder to add the next one in a month and so forth while dropping what doesn't work well for you.

For this exercise, you'll need your goals at the forefront of your mind as you choose your structure.

You will need structure for goal setting, planning, and scheduling. This means scheduling time to review your goals and vision and developing new plans of action. Your plan, of course, needs to allow some time for the intervention of Holy Spirit and fly by the seat of your pants. You might need to experiment a bit so that this works for you.

You will also need a structure for acquiring new strategies. This might be best done by working with peers, a coach, or a mentor. You can also work alone by brainstorming, recording dreams, and mind mapping. God will give you awesome help in this department as well. You might want to schedule this on a monthly basis, perhaps using part of a day.

You need a system for tracking and measuring. I'm all over this aspect of success strategies. I love metrics and analytics; you may not. Tracking provides clear feedback on what works and what doesn't. Decide on one or two things you care about and develop an easy system for tracking.

You need accountability. Almost all of us perform better in relationships than we do solo. An accountability partner will help you set clear objectives and actions and check in with you at a predetermined date. You can both see whether you took action. If yes, it's party time; if not, brainstorm how to do better or reprioritize and recommit to taking action.

You need reminders. You need a system to set them up and deploy as needed. Todoist, a phone calendar, Google calendar, sticky notes, or a personal assistant all work.

You need people. This can take the form of coaches, consultants, assistants, employees, subcontractors, partners, mentors, or mastermind groups.

HOMEWORK:

The best structure comes from a balance of social with others helping you and solo when you don't need anyone else to get it done. Choose at least one social support and one solo support to implement. Feel free to invent your own system.

ONWARD AND UPWARD!

You've finished your vision. You have a solid marketing plan. You have a strategy for reaching your goals and maximizing your time. And you know how to keep going.

Now you just need to follow your plans and continue to invite God into the process so he can help you pivot and seize opportunities as they arise.

Some of you just needed to solidify your foundations so that you can make the needed changes in your business for a less stressful and more supernatural business or ministry. We wish you all the best and send our blessings with you as you go out and conquer your mountain.

We also know that some of you who picked up this book need more help with putting all the pieces in place to begin to build a business or ministry that aligns with your God-given vision. We'd love to help you with that.

We have a year-long class with modules on everything from websites to email responders to product development to marketing to scaling and more. In addition to the lessons, we have live Q&A times and co-working sessions where we dive in with you and help you sort the technological aspects. You can get off on the right foot with your business or ministry and avoid a lot of the frustration and loneliness of building on your own.

Check out https://supernaturalbiz.com/?wpam_id=1 for more details on this.

Thank you for reading our book, and we hope to see you in class some time very soon!

Structure

List ideas for social and solo support to implement, then circle the ones you are going to implement and describe how you're going to be diligent with the implementation.

Social support

1.

2.

3.

4.

5.

Solo support

1.

2.

3.

4.

5.

How are you going to be diligent with the implementation:

Endnotes

1   Merriam-Webster, s.v. "vision (n.)," accessed November 14, 2021, https://www.merriam-webster.com/dictionary/vision.

2   Lewis Carroll, Alice in Wonderland, (New York: Macmillan & Company, 1865) 71–72, http://www.open-bks.com/alice-71-72.html.

3   I first learned this technique at Splankna training in Denver, CO April 2011

4   Zig Ziglar, "Selling is not something you do to someone, it's something you do for someone," Facebook, February 28, 2013, https://www.facebook.com/ZigZiglar/posts/selling-is-not-something-you-do-to-someone-its-something-you-do-for-someone-zig-/10151463724482863.

5   Although this saying is sometimes credited to Mark Batterson, it was around for years before he wrote his first book. It is considered a truism of the Christian faith by many, and the source is unknown.

6   Wikipedia, s.v. "kairos," last modified November 1, 2021, 1:09, https://en.wikipedia.org/wiki/Kairos.

7   Albert Einstein, Letter of condolence to the Besso family, 1955.

8   Encyclopaedia Britannica online, s.v., "Re: Egyptian god," accessed October 29, 2021, https://www.britannica.com/topic/Re.

9   Stephen R. Covey, The 7 Habits of Highly Effective People: Powerful Lessons in Personal Change (New York City: Simon & Schuster, 2013).

10   Steven Pressfield, The War of Art (New York City: Black Irish Entertainment, 2002), 37.

About Alice Briggs

In her three main businesses, Alice helps others to achieve their goals and dreams, removing the head trash that gets in the way. She's intrigued by the connection between emotional and spiritual health and physical well-being.

She runs three businesses as an artist, inner healing practitioner, and book designer. She's written more than thirty books about art and healing.

She's partnered with Seneca to help you ditch your road blocks so that you can move forward in your business and life. She knows that your biggest difficulty may be dealing with what's between your own ears.

Get rid of your head trash and the sky's the limit!

AliceArlene.com

EmotionalAndSpiritualHealing.com

KingdomCovers.com

About Seneca Schurbon

Founder of Freedom Flowers, Seneca Schurbon started making essences intuitively when she was a little girl, and has been in business of one kind or another since age five. From freelancing to consulting; from client work to ecommerce and information products; she has been there, done that.

Now Freedom Flowers has production hubs in four countries and growing! Seneca also writes extensively about health and spirituality and is the author of seven books.

In her business classes, Seneca believes it's not what you know, but Who you know. The best strategy comes from God. She helps you break it down, ask the right questions, and helps put abstract answers into concrete plans of action.

It's ancient path meets information super highway!

Freedom-Flowers.com

Join the Challenge or take the Class

SupernaturalBiz.com

Coupon good for the Challenge only: Iboughtthebook

Made in the USA
Middletown, DE
14 June 2022

67110723R00057